Time Capsule Ghost Stories

Francesca Kyanda

BookLeaf
Publishing

India | USA | UK

Presentation by *BookLeaf Publishing*

Web: www.bookleafpub.com

E-mail: info@bookleafpub.com

ISBN: 9789357447140

First edition 2022

DEDICATION

To Sophia Kunkel, the whole reason this collection exists. Literally. She made me promise to finish.

ACKNOWLEDGEMENT

Firstly, I have to thank Sophia, who encouraged me to write this collection and for freaking out every time I wrote something new. To Nour and Riya and Jaidah, who loved every single word and were my first real audience. Y'all are straight-up baddies. My parents, who prayed for me, never limited any writing goal I had and bought me notebook after notebook in exchange for me penning the next bestseller. I'm getting there, I promise. To everyone who helped me make a memory: you are loved, remembered and I've probably written a poem or two about it. To anyone with time capsule ghost stories of their own: release them into the air. Trap them on paper. One day, they will leave you.

PREFACE

This collection is a clash of nonfiction and magical realism, in which I substitute ghosts and memories for people. I'm aware that the existence of ghosts is a centuries-old debate. I'm not really adding anything to that, I'm writing things the way I remember.

(s)he loves me,
(s)he loves me not

have you ever seen
a sunflower and
been overcome
with the desire
to approach it
and tell it to bow
to the rain that
nourishes it
tell it that is
nothing without
the rain
have you ever seen
a sunflower and
wanted to end
something beautiful
so you yank it
from its roots
as it screams and
pluck out petals
one by
one by
one

until it is
nothing but a
bleeding bud
and still it lives
have you ever seen
a sunflower and
snapped its
neck
and liked it

tear-full

I found a tear on
my face one afternoon
and did not know
what it was doing
there so I licked at
the corner of my
mouth where it
had dripped
until more
overcame me
and I was a
monsoon

lemons out of lemonade

I feel too much/ what I mean is/ I roll my emotions like lemon drops/ hide them in the lining of my cheeks/ crush them between my teeth/my tongue shredded like fringe/sometimes I wonder if I taste of citrus/or cancer/if my tears would be bitter or sweet/if they'd cause drastic erosion in the atmosphere/if I could end the world/could I refuse that kind of power/he did

if only

He's got a whole room
in my house of memories.
Knocks over lamps, turns up rugs.
He's not a jerk in my head, just
adorable and
clumsy. Always
blushing. He's like
a bit of
scraped skin
on your knee:
white, vulnerable.

that mirror in harry potter but warped

writing poems about
people who exist is taking
their corpses from graves,
having tea with their ghosts
and writing their stories.
maybe it's not right but
it has to be done
for the truth.

what's his name, he has the dreamcoat and the brothers

he's not the type to run
from demons. the little ones,
he'd chase around the playground
and tickle them until they squealed.
he'd sit between their legs and
let them braid his hair, grow it out
long special for them.
he's not the type to run from
demons, he'd tell them stories
and take their pictures, tell them
they look beautiful and make them blush.
storybook wonderful, assassin dangerous.

warning label
written on my cheek

don't hang the moon for me.
don't trap me in your picture frame,
press rosebuds to my cheeks.
your kiss is fishhook to the lip,
pulling, why can't you practice
catch and release of me?

get thee behind, foul blondie

what led you to confessional?
did she stuff her heart underneath
the floorboards and you hear it
in your ears as it was your own?
were you lured, looking for fresh blood,
a new girl who'll purple her knees
for your pleasure?
you expected me to call you
weary traveler, waymaker, explorer
of realms, sing your praises as hymns?
there isn't enough holy water
for you, she drank it all to excuse
her sins.

pov: your ghost follows me around

your ghost follows me around,
makes me question the reality
around me. your memory wants
to be dug up, made museum artifact.
you beg for your legacy to be
pedestaled in bronze.
once, you joked that I made you
up in my mind, that you didn't exist.
this Twilight Zone what-if is more
my style.

imaginary first date

I am plotting all the ways
your blood can spill. if the
bruises on my heart start to
look like your hands, if
I wake up with your name
on my lips.
what are your
pressure points?
I can see you're already
scanning me for weaknesses.
my hands have been known
to be defenders, curled up
tight to be fighting things.
I fight because I am tired
of people leaving with
bits of me on their tongue.
I'm only violent when provoked,
a terrified wild animal afraid
of being deemed as small
and defendless
and
easy to
conquer.

he's not a ghost but he makes a good poem

He is a hungry mouth,
lips dripping gasoline,
looking for a spark, a
flicker of flame, teeth
like pieces of the moon
that makes a crescent
yearn to be whole again.
He is a hollowed out body,
once lean and agile, now
curved into question mark,
all knotted and wanting.
He is daydream made flesh
and grin, wobbly and layered
with scars. He is jumping fences
and picking locks, finding other
ways to get what he wants.
He is the poem that bursts
from a dried-up pen after there
were no more words to say into
a slit-mouth silence.

little red riding wolf

The rose around my neck died,
and I wrapped myself in thorns
to let people know I was a
brambled thing, uprooted,
overgrown.
Snapping twigs in this
fractured fairytale forest,
ear to the ground for
threatening earthquakes.
People still want to hike
here though, chopping through
branches, climbing up dying bark,
yet I'm too closed off to feel
the tread of their footsteps.
Don't they know it's
sacrilegious to trample upon
blessed ground?
Prophecy tells that this
forest was destined to welcome
the right people or no one at all.

i'm sorry, i got it on your sneakers, i hope it washes out

I pull back the fabric of
my clothing and let you look
at this raw, bleeding, beating
thing in my chest.
I let you prod the cardiac tissue
without any hesitation.
This thing that drops blood
on clean pages, that squeezes
tight in my chest, with the
constant torn tissue and
never healing scars, is all
that I have to offer.
Hope brims in my eyes,
and I watch as you sweep
your gaze over it. You
shake you head, step back
and leave, letting me
button my shirt back up.
First to give, never to receive.

you don't know
what you've done

I am a tangerine, the abandoned
old skin you peeled and peeled
until I was bare and you dropped
it to the floor, crunching it with your heel.
Your eager fingers shaky, even careless,
picking away at my parts. Nothing too
dry for you, my fruit offers thirst quenched,
the dull of hunger pains finally silenced.
You take a bite, juice dribbling over
your lips, down your chin and wrists.
You sigh with relief as the juice
travels down your ungrateful throat.
You continue, juice still sweet,
slices bursting between your teeth
with the right amount of pressure.
It gives you pleasure, the relief that
the taste of the fruit gives you,
doesn't it? After all, you were
so hungry and the tangerine was
sitting right there, out in the open.
No one else was watching and
you'd needed food for days.

No one would mind; it didn't
seem to belong to anyone.
So you took it.
Maybe it didn't belong to anybody,
but it certainly didn't belong to you.
It is your fault that your stomach
growls that; find another food source.
"But the juice was so good," you say.
"The way it dropped down my chin
and made me feel whole."
Well, there rests the mangled,
devoured fruit in your stomach.
It has no voice, you stole it.
It has no body, you robbed it.
It has no say in any of this, you
drained it of all the juice
it could provide.
I'm glad I could satisfy
your hunger.

I came to resolve his sins, Father

people shouldn't be
allowed to give me
good memories alongside
the bad ones.
I shouldn't remember your
smile right before I
remember how you screamed
at me.
Your memory doesn't even
deserve to be pure, yet
here I am.

they are not gods

it's been seventeen years and I
still don't know how not to make
people into churches.
Build pews and altars,
light incense and murmur
prayers in the quiet.
I didn't know that I wasn't
supposed to annoint you, kiss
your feet, give offerings. I make
you into a deity that you're not,
praise and worship the ground
you walk on.
I advise you not to make
people into true religion.
See them as people, human,
not gods deserving psalms
and rosary beads.
They are not gods, the people I love.
So take down the altars and see
them, not your delusion.

time of death: 11:59 PM

nothing brings back memories
like looking at your picture
in the middle of the night,
glasses off, the picture
fuzzy until I hold it right
up to my eyes, shoulders
up to my ears, the most
eye contact we've made
in a whole year.

lemons, lime and plenty of time

I've had a year to turn lemons
into lemonade. at least there's
no hurting anyone. no fighting.
no yelling or screaming. but
sometimes I add too much
sugar and miss the
gorgeous, fierce person I
thought I met that day
in September. sometimes
I drink the lemon juice
straight and force myself
to reconcile that
you're just bitterness
and pulp.